Big-Enough Anna

❄ The Little Sled Dog Who Braved the Arctic ❄

WRITTEN BY **Pam Flowers** with **Ann Dixon**
ILLUSTRATED BY **Bill Farnsworth**

ALASKA NORTHWEST BOOKS®
Anchorage, Alaska ❄ Portland, Oregon

Anna was the smallest and youngest puppy in her litter, born in a winter deep with snow. Walls of white edged the path to the dog lot, where the puppies snuggled against their mother.

Anna's owner, a dog musher named Pam, checked frequently on the new arrivals. That first month she visited the puppies often, talking to them, petting them, and watching them play.

Soon they wriggled with happiness to see Pam coming.

*O*ne day, when the puppies were about four weeks old, Anna peered over the edge of the doghouse. She wanted to go exploring, but her three-inch legs weren't nearly long enough to reach the ground.

Plop! Anna scrambled headfirst into the snow.

Roald and Sojo, her brother and sister, were not so brave. They waited several days before following Anna out into the big, white world.

*A*t three months, Anna was the first to wear a dog harness.
Pam attached a string tied to a twig for her to drag around. When
the other puppies saw Anna, they wanted to practice being sled
dogs, too. Soon all three were pulling twigs, then sticks, then
small logs.

When they were five months old, the puppies tried mushing for
the first time.

Each week, Pam increased the distance they traveled: one mile,
two miles, three. By six months all the puppies could pull a sled
for five miles.

Little Anna always pulled the hardest.

*T*he puppies didn't know it, but Pam was preparing for a long and difficult expedition. Next winter she hoped to become the first woman to mush alone across the Arctic. It would take about six months, she thought, to travel 2,500 miles by dogsled.

Pam decided to let the puppies train with the older dogs. She watched them carefully to see if they were strong enough to join the expedition team.

Anna was still the smallest dog in the lot. But she always tried hard and paid attention.

Anna just loved to run!

One winter day they met another team training on the trail. When the musher stopped to chat, Pam told him about her plan to mush dogs across the Arctic.

"Get rid of that one," he said, pointing to Anna. "She's too little to pull much weight."

"Anna's tougher than she looks," Pam argued. "She works hard and never quits. That's more important than size."

The man shook his head. "She won't last a week," he muttered, and mushed off.

"Don't listen to him," Pam told Anna. "I think you're plenty big enough."

Several months later, when the winter sun returned to the Arctic, training ended and the expedition began. A crowd of well-wishers gathered to see them off.

The puppies were thirteen months old now. Each had earned a place on the team. They ran in back, where all young sled dogs start out.

Anna was still the smallest. But she worked the hardest. She always kept her tug line straight and listened when Pam spoke.

Anna ran so well that Pam did something she'd never done before. She let a puppy try running in the lead, the most important position. She moved Anna up front, right next to Douggie, a big, strong nine-year-old who had led many trips in the Arctic.

*P*oor Douggie! Anna was excited to be up front, but she didn't know what to do. Douggie had to show her everything: how to follow commands, how to find a trail, how to tell if ice was too thin for safe crossing.

When Pam called "Gee!" Anna ran straight ahead, until Douggie pushed her to the right.

When Pam called "Haw!" Anna lunged to the right, until Douggie pulled her to the left.

It was hard work for Douggie. He was a patient teacher.

It was hard work for Anna, too. But she learned quickly: first "Gee!" and "Haw!"; then "Whoa!" to stop and "Let's go!" to begin.

One morning, about halfway through the expedition, a herd of caribou trotted by just as Pam was harnessing the dogs.

For once, dependable Douggie disobeyed. Before Pam could stop him, Douggie ran after the caribou and disappeared into the hills.

The next morning Douggie still hadn't returned to camp.

Pam grew worried. Was Douggie all right? Would they find him? Without a lead dog, the expedition could not continue.

She studied Anna. Could such a small, young dog possibly take over as leader?

"What do you say?" Pam asked, scratching behind Anna's ears. "Are you big enough to lead this team on your own?"

*F*or the next week and a half, with Anna in lead, they searched the hills and valleys for Douggie.

Day after day, Anna led the team. Mile after mile after mile. On the tenth day, Pam gave up hope of ever seeing Douggie again.

Without food or water, he could not survive. Sadly, she decided it was time to quit searching.

Still, there was hope for the expedition. Anna had done so well leading on her own, there was a chance they could finish.

*A*s they packed up to leave, a snowmobiler came by. Someone had found Douggie!

The dogs seemed to understand. With Anna leading, they raced to meet Douggie. But when they reached him, the team realized something was wrong.

Douggie was thin and exhausted. He didn't seem to recognize them, but simply stood still, his eyes listless and dazed.

The team sniffed him gently. Cautiously, they wagged their tails.

Douggie looked at his teammates, as if waking from a bad dream. Slowly, very slowly, his tail started to wag as well.

*A*fter several days of rest and plenty to eat, Douggie was able to travel again. But he couldn't lead for long without becoming tired. Now big, strong Douggie needed little Anna to help him.

Near the end of the expedition, they began crossing a frozen sea so wide that it would take about ten days to reach the other side.

The team made good time the first day. Then the weather turned unusually warm.

The frozen sea beneath them began to melt. The dogs had to work extra hard to pull through several inches of slush. Each day it became harder to travel.

Most days it rained. Soon the ice was dotted with holes hidden beneath the slush. If it melted much more there would be no ice left to travel on. Then they would fall into the sea and drown.

To make matters even worse, they were almost out of food. Pam had to cut meals in half before they ran out completely. Only Douggie received full portions. Even with full meals, Douggie wasn't strong enough to pull. He walked beside Anna and simply tried to keep up.

Everyone was wet, exhausted, and hungry. Could they make it to the other side?

Anna got tired, but she didn't give up. She kept right on slogging through the slush. She guided the team around thin ice and jumped bravely over areas of open water.

If Anna can keep going, I can too, thought Pam.

The team seemed to agree. On and on they trudged, following Anna.

Finally, on the fourteenth day, they saw land. Closer and closer, Anna picked out a path through the slush. Soon they were just a hundred feet—a hundred steps!—from shore.

*S*uddenly, *splash!* Anna disappeared into a hole.

The hole was filled with frigid seawater, churning like a whirlpool. Anna scrambled frantically to keep her head above water, her front paws thrashing at the ice as she struggled to pull herself out.

Pam rushed forward to help. *Crack!* The ice beneath her began to break. If Pam fell in, too, they would both die. She had to retreat to the sled.

The water was so cold, Anna couldn't last much longer.

Douggie was still weak, but he was their only hope. Pam yelled: "Haw, Douggie! Haw!"

Could he do it? Could he save Anna?

*D*ouggie understood. Somehow he found the strength to start pulling.

Anna kept trying to claw her way onto the ice. Douggie pulled, but he was too weak to drag her out on his own.

Suddenly, the other dogs jumped into action. They strained at the rope with Douggie. Slowly, inch by inch, they pulled Anna out of the sea.

For a moment Pam held her breath, wondering, *Is Anna too frightened to go on?*

The moment passed. Anna shook herself off and stepped back into lead, as if nothing had even happened.

Pam shook her head in amazement. What a tough, brave little dog!

"Let's go!" Pam called and off they mushed. Soon they were standing on dry, solid land.

Many miles later they reached the end of their long journey.

With Pam whooping and hollering on the back of the sled, little Anna led the team into town, where the mayor and a crowd waited to congratulate them. Pam shook hands with everyone, saying, "Thank you! Thank you!"

When the excitement died down, Pam sat quietly with her dogs. "I'm so proud of you all," she said. "What a great team!" They wagged their tails and she knew they understood.

Pam turned to Anna. "You're still small," she said. "But you're a lead dog now. I can count on you to never give up.

"You're plenty big enough, Anna!" ❄

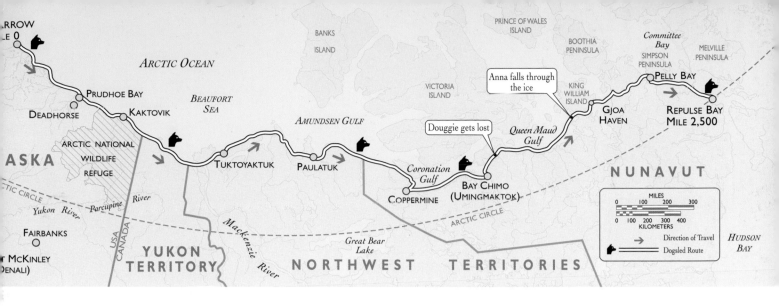

❊ EPILOGUE ❊

On February 14, 1993, Pam Flowers and her eight sled dogs left Barrow, Alaska, to mush across the top of North America, 2,500 miles east to Repulse Bay, Canada. They reached their goal almost a year later, on January 9, 1994, after numerous hardships, challenges, and setbacks. All eight dogs finished the expedition in good health and good spirits.

ABOVE: PAM AND HER BEST FRIENDS IN THE NORTH AMERICAN ARCTIC, WITH ANNA AND DOUGGIE IN LEAD.

LEFT: ANNA (LEFT) RESTS WITH TEAMMATES LUCY AND ROBERT.

In finishing the expedition, Pam became the first woman to traverse the North American Arctic alone. You can read a full account of Pam's expedition in *Alone across the Arctic: One Woman's Epic Journey by Dog Team* by Pam Flowers with Ann Dixon.

To Anna, who saved the expedition, and to her seven teammates,
who worked together to make this journey a success.
— P. F.

To my Aunts Carole (1936–1999), LaVerne, Lois, and Mary.
— A. D.

To my wife, Debbie, and my daughters, Allison and Caitlin,
who, with me, experienced Alaska for the first time.
— B. F.

LIBRARY OF CONGRESS CATALOGING-IN-PUBLICATION DATA

Flowers, Pam.
   Big-enough Anna : the little sled dog who braved the Arctic / written by Pam Flowers with Ann Dixon ; illustrated by Bill Farnsworth.
      p. cm.
   Summary: Describes how a small dog became the lead dog as her musher, Pam Flowers, prepared for and made her historic journey alone across the North American Arctic.
   ISBN 0-88240-577-2 (hb) — ISBN 0-88240-580-2 (sb)
   1. Sled dogs—Alaska—Biography—Juvenile literature. 2. Dogsledding—Alaska—Juvenile literature. 3. Dogsledding—Canada, Northern—Juvenile literature. 4. Dogsledding—Arctic regions—Juvenile literature. 5. Flowers, Pam—Journeys—Alaska—Juvenile literature. 6. Flowers, Pam—Journeys—Canada, Northern— Juvenile literature. 7. Flowers, Pam—Journeys—Arctic regions—Juvenile literature. [1. Sled dogs. 2. Dogsledding. 3. Dogs. 4. Flowers, Pam. 5. Voyages and travels. 6. Arctic regions—Description and travel.] I. Dixon, Ann. II. Farnsworth, Bill, ill. III. Title.

SF428.7.F59 2003
636.73—dc21   2003045200

Alaska Northwest Books®
An imprint of Graphic Arts Center Publishing Company
P.O. Box 10306, Portland, Oregon 97296-0306
503-226-2402 / www.gacpc.com

Fifth hardbound printing 2006 • Sixth softbound printing 2006

President: Charles M. Hopkins
Associate Publisher: Douglas A. Pfeiffer
Editorial Staff: Timothy W. Frew, Tricia Brown, Jean Andrews, Kathy Howard, Jean Bond-Slaughter
Production Staff: Richard L. Owsiany, Susan Dupere
Editor: Michelle McCann
Book and cover design: Andrea L. Boven, Boven Design Studio, Inc.
Mapmaker: Gray Mouse Graphics

Printed in Hong Kong